Pee-Yew!

The Stinkiest, Smelliest Animals, Insects, and Plants on Earth!

Mike Artell

A GOOD YEAR BOOK™

Good Year Books
Tucson, Arizona

Good Year Books

Our titles are available for most basic curriculum subjects plus many enrichment areas. For more Good Year Books, contact your local bookseller or educational dealer. For a complete catalog with information about other Good Year Books, please contact:

Good Year Books
P.O. Box 91858
Tucson, AZ 85752-1858
www.goodyearbooks.com

Cover Design: Performance Design
Text Design: Performance Design
Drawings: Mike Artell

A GOOD YEAR BOOK™

Photo Credits

Front cover: Johnny Lye, ant; Mike Artell, green stinkbug; Golden Egg Bug, and Caterpillar Hunter; David B. Rickman, millipede; Ericka Thorpe, Zebra Swallowtail Caterpillar; James Lin, stinkbug; Samuel Goldstein, sundew; Kevin Rohr, turkey vulture; Patti Adair, earwig. **Back cover:** Mike Artell, walking stick. **Interior:** 6: Philip Sasser, stock.xchng. 9: Bram van Dijk, stock.xchng. 10: Jenny Hardie, stock.xchng. 11: Martin Will, fotolia.com. 13: Courtesy of Pacific Northwest National Laboratory. 18: Trisha Shears, stock.xchng. 19: (top) Christian Simon, stock.xchng, (bottom) Györvári Gábor, stock.xchng. 20: Geoff Kuchera, iStockPhoto.com. 22: Tomaz Levstek, iStockPhoto.com. 24: Peter 'Langy' Langshaw, stock.xchng. 25: Virag Vig, stock.xchng. 26: Kevin Rohr, stock.xchng. 27: Matthew Maaskant, stock.xchng. 29: D. Merton. Crow Copyright. Department of Conservation, New Zealand, 2001. 30: Laura Erickson, Binoculars.com. 30: Jeff LeClere, herpnet.net. 31: National Parks Service. 32: James Lin, chumby.net, stock.xchng. 33: Courtesy of Mike Artell. 34: (top) Clemson University, USDA Cooperative Extension Slide Series, insectimages.com, (bottom) Susan Ellis, insectimages.com. 35: Michael Ferro, Louisiana State Arthropod Museum. 36-40: Courtesy of Mike Artell. 41: Hays Cummins, Miami University. 42: Scott Bauer, USDA. 43: (top) Courtesy of Mike Artell; (middle) Scott Bauer, USDA; (bottom) Scott Bauer, USDA. 45: (top) ricsike, stock.xchng; (bottom) Johnny Lye, iStockPhoto.com. 46: Keith Weller, USDA. 48: David Coder, iStockPhoto.com. 50: Courtesy of Mike Artell. 51: (top) Matthew Cole, iStockPhoto.com; (middle) Courtesy of Mike Artell; (bottom) David B. Rickman, New Mexico State University, Las Cruces, USDA. 52: Richard C. Hoyer, Birding and Natural History Tour Leader, wingsbirds.com/leaders/hoyer.htm. 53: Chartchai Meesangnin, iStockPhoto.com. 54: Patti Adair, stock.xchng. 55: (top) Clemson University, USDA Cooperative Extension Slide Series, insectimages.com; (bottom) Whitney Cranshaw, Colorado State University, insectimages.com. 56: Robyn Waayers. 57: Zie, iStockPhoto.com. 58: Chartchai Meesangnin, iStockPhoto.com. 59: (top) Clemson University, USDA Cooperative Extension Slide Series, insectimages.com, (bottom) Ron Billings, Texas Forest Service, insectimages.com. 60: (top) Diane Miller, stock.xchng, (bottom) Ericka Thorpe, stock.xchng. 61: E.L. Manigault slide collection, Department of Entomology, Soils & Plant Sciences, Clemson University. 62: Courtesy of Mike Artell. 63: Courtesy of Mike Artell. 64: Pam Roth, CreatingOnline.com, stock.xchng. 65: U.S. Fish and Wildlife Service. 68: Cambridge 2000. 69: Wilbert Hetterscheid. 70: Cambridge 2000. 71: (left) Lisa Harris Tetzaff, (right) David Riggs, (bottom) Cambridge 2000. 72: John C. Carter. 73: Taylor F. Lockwood. 74: Taylor F. Lockwood. 75: TomVolkfungi.net. 76: (top) Stockert, National Parks Service; (inset) Matt Goff, sitkanature.org; (bottom) ©Mark Turner, Turner Photographics. 77: (top) Dr. Robert Beall, Flathead Valley Community College, (bottom) National Parks Service. 78: Henriette Kress, henriettesherbal.com. 79: (top) Samuel Goldstein, (bottom) Kevin Miller, stock.xchng. 80: Daniel Greenhouse. 81: Herbex Ltd. Fiji, goodnoni.biz. 82: JohnHarveyPhoto.com. 83: Pamela Trewatha. 84-85: Courtesy of Mike Artell. 86: (top) United States Department of the Interior, (bottom) Jan Rihak, iStockPhoto.com. 87: (top) Dave Dyet, stock.xchng, (bottom) Pamela Hodson, iStockPhoto.com. 88: Andrei Tchernov, iStockPhoto.com. 96: Courtesy of Mike Artell.

WARNING!

Don't read this book . . .

. . . unless you want to know about plants, animals, and insects that smell bad and do disgusting things.

You do want to know about those things?
OK, don't say we didn't warn you . . .

Contents

Contents

Introduction

Some plants, animals, and insects are so stinky and smelly that they deserve a whole book of their own. And now they have one! In this book, you'll learn about some pretty stinky animals, insects, and plants. But remember: Even though they smell bad, all are important to life on earth.

Many plants use their stinky smells to attract bees and flies. The bees and flies spread the plants' pollen, which fertilizes the plants so the plants can produce fruit. The seeds from the fruit create new plants.

Animals and insects often use strong smells to attract mates or to let other animals and insects know that they have moved into the area. When animals find mates, they are able to reproduce, and life can go on. That's why even stinky smells are important.

Are you ready for a REALLY SMELLY adventure? Good, let's get started. But before you turn the page, do the following:

 **Take your thumb and put it on the side of your nose.**

 **Take your index finger and put it on the other side of your nose.**

 **Pinch your nose closed so you can't smell anything.**

 **Got it? OK, turn the page . . .**

Part I

Humans Smell, in More Ways Than One

For a long time, scientists didn't understand much about our human sense of smell and how it works. Recently, however, they have made new discoveries that have helped them better understand how our sense of smell is connected to our other senses, to our memories, and to the way we understand the world.

Here's what happens when you smell something:

As you breathe in, air passes over millions of cilia inside the upper part of your nose. Cilia are tiny little hairs covered with a wet coating called mucous. This mucous catches the chemicals in the air and dissolves them.

Each cilia cell has hundreds of receptors. A receptor is a part of the cilia cell that checks the air for chemicals it recognizes. If the receptor recognizes a chemical, it tells your brain. Your brain takes information from all the receptors and then decides whether what you're smelling is nice or nasty. So even though it seems weird, your brain does a lot of the work of smelling. It all happens very fast, and every time you breathe, your cilia, receptors, and brain go through the whole process again.

SMELLY FACT

Our sense of smell affects the way things taste. When we say something has a good "flavor," we're really saying that it has a good taste and a good smell, because "flavor" is a combination of both.

You Smell, Too!

Smells are important because they warn us of danger—such as when something is burning. Smells can also help us find food. Have you ever smelled cookies baking? Smells can even let us know when someone else is nearby. For example, if you smell perfume or aftershave lotion, there's a pretty good chance that someone else is in the room with you. Many years ago, when people lived in caves, a good sense of smell helped cavemen and their families locate food and avoid danger.

Even though most of us don't live in caves anymore, we still use our sense of smell every day. When you wake up in the morning, you might smell bacon cooking in the kitchen. Maybe when you're waiting for the school bus, you smell the smoky exhaust from old cars and trucks on the street. Your sense of smell might also tell you when it's time to change the litter in your cat's litter box! Try making a list of all the ways you use your sense of smell each day.

Many animals and plants could not survive without their sense of smell. This book will introduce you to those living things and show you how all of them are important to life on earth . . . even though they smell bad. Have fun, and don't forget to hold your nose as you read, because everything about this book stinks!

Scientists tell us that everyone has a unique scent. But in addition to our natural odor, think of all the ways we add smells to ourselves:

Aftershave

Deodorant

Perfume

Mouthwash

Powder

Lotions and creams

SMELLY FACT
The fear that you smell bad is called autodysomphobia.

On rare occasions, people can't help the way they smell. For example, there is a disease called trimethylaminuria that makes a person smell like fish, no matter how much he or she washes or bathes. But it's very rare. Fewer than 500 people have ever been reported to have this disease.

If you want to know more about human body odors, visit these Web sites:

http://serendip.brynmawr.edu/biology/b103/f02/web2/mbrown.html
http://chnm.gmu.edu/features/sidelights/whoinventedbo.html
http://atoz.iqhealth.com/HealthAnswers/encyclopedia/HTMLfiles/3190.html

SMELLY FACT

Stinky Water—For many years in the city of Patan, Nepal, there were no working water pipes, so people lined up to get drinking water from two water spouts. The water from those spouts is still said to be the stinkiest water anyone has ever smelled. It contains high levels of acid and ammonia as well as other chemicals. Somehow over time, the people have gotten used to the smell. Fortunately, in the last few years an increasing number of people in Patan have gotten access to clean water that has been piped in.

Odor Fatigue

When you exercise hard, your muscles can get tired, or fatigued. Your sense of smell can get fatigued too. It's called odor fatigue.

Have you ever walked into a house or a building that smells bad, but the people inside don't notice the smell anymore? That's because the "smell cells" in their noses have already sent the smell information for that particular odor to their brains. For them to be aware of the odor again, the cells have to wait until the odor particles have dissolved or been swept away by their breathing. Then the odor particles can attach themselves to the "smell cells" again. But it takes time for that to happen. In the meantime, the people in the house or building are wondering why you're holding your nose when everything smells just fine to them.

Artificial Noses

There are thousands of people who have a problem with their sense of smell. They either cannot smell anything (called anosmia) or they have a difficult time detecting smells.

On the battlefield and in chemical plants, people have to be alert for the possibility of dangerous chemicals in the air. Because many dangerous chemicals have no odor, these people could find out too late that the air they are breathing is not safe.

Scientists know about these problems and they are developing artificial noses that can detect odors people cannot smell. Some of these artificial noses use computers and electronics and others use dyes that change colors when certain chemicals are in the air. Some of these noses are hundreds of times more sensitive than human noses.

This scientist is working with an artificial nose. It is in the clear box on top of the computer.

SMELLY FACT

In 2004 scientists at Cranfield University in England used an artificial nose to test fourteen cheeses. They named Vieux Boulogne, a soft cheese from northern France, the smelliest cheese on earth.

Part II

Smelly Animals

Smells Are Important to Animals, Too!

Animals that have big ears can usually hear better than other animals. Animals with large eyes can often see things that other animals can't see. The same is true of smells. The more receptor cells an animal has in its nose, the more smells it can sense.

BRR...

Most other mammals have a much better sense of smell than humans. Scientists are still trying to determine how many receptor cells each kind of animal has, but at this time they think humans have about 5 to 40 million receptors in their noses. That sounds like a lot, until you realize that rabbits have about 20 million. Have you ever watched a rabbit's nose twitching? The rabbit is constantly sniffing the air to test it for the smell of food or predators—or maybe other rabbits! Rabbits need big ears and a great sense of smell, because lots of other animals like to have rabbits for dinner.

Dogs are incredible smellers. They can have 125 to 225 million receptor cells in their noses. That's why rescue teams use dogs to help search for people who are lost in the woods or who have been buried by snow. Some dogs, like bloodhounds, have such a wonderful sense of smell that they can detect smells even other dogs can't sense. And researchers have found that wolves can smell certain scents that are more than a mile away.

SMELLY FACT

Have you ever seen squirrels kissing? One of the ways little Belding's Ground Squirrels identify other family members is by sniffing each other's facial glands. They have to get very close to sniff each other's faces and it looks like they're kissing. Awwww . . .

Do your feet smell? Yes! If you're a fly.

Flies can actually taste things with their feet! Flies have little sensors in their feet that help them taste what they walk on. If they land on something and decide that it's tasty, they'll stick their mouth parts on it and taste it again.

MMM... SOMETHING SMELLS GOOD!

FLICK

FLICK

TAKE YOUR SHOES OFF AND TASTE THIS CAKE. IT'S DELICIOUS!

SMELLY FACT

Flies are the only flying insect with two wings. All other flying insects have four wings.

Can you smell with your tongue? Yes! If you're a snake.

Inside a snake's mouth is its Jacobson's organ. Snakes use this organ to help smell their surroundings. As snakes flick their tongues into the air, tiny odor particles collect on the surface of their tongues. When the snake brings its tongue back into its mouth, the tongue fits into the little place inside its mouth that contains the Jacobson's organ. This organ "smells" the odor particles. Then, the snake can decide if there's some prey or a predator nearby.

Dogs Can Smell Cancer

Scientists have found that dogs can use their incredible sense of smell to tell if a person has cancer. In one experiment, scientists trained dogs by using body fluids from cancer patients, people who were ill with diseases other than cancer, and healthy people. The dogs had to identify the fluids from the cancer patients by lying next to the dish holding the fluids. By smell alone, the dogs could pick the fluids from the cancer patient more than 40 percent of the time. Two of the dogs were able to pick the cancer patients' fluids more than 55 percent of the time.

In another test, all the dogs identified a container of fluids as being from a cancer patient even though doctors had not identified any cancer in that person. After they did more tests, the doctor discovered cancer on the person's kidney.

Cats Depend on Smells

If you have a pet cat, it probably loves the way you rub it and scratch it. But when a cat rubs up against you, it's probably not just because it loves you back. More than likely, your cat is "marking" you. Cats have scent glands around their mouths, heads, and tails. When your cat rubs up against you, it is leaving some of its scent on you. It's telling other cats, "This human belongs to me." Cats also like to rub against chairs, table legs, and other things that it wants other cats to know it "owns."

SMELLY FACT
Many animals have scent glands in their paw pads. When they scratch a tree, they leave a little of their scent behind.

Skunks

The best-known smelly animal is a skunk. Most skunks are about the size of a house cat. They usually live in holes in the ground, but they will also live under houses, in hollow logs, or in piles of wood.

Skunks will eat just about anything. They like fruit and nuts, but they will also eat beetles, insects, and lizards. They'll even eat dead animals on the road. **Yuck!**

Skunks prefer to live alone, but they will share a space with other skunks when they are raising babies or when they huddle together in a warm place during a cold winter. Skunks are most active at night.

SMELLY FACT
The spotted skunk does a handstand as it squirts its scent.

WHAT TO DO IF YOU GET SQUIRTED

If you or your pet gets squirted by a skunk, you'll want to wash the stinky stuff off of you (or them) as quickly as you can. Here's a recipe for a de-skunking deodorant wash that you can use. Be sure to get an adult to help you mix the ingredients:

1 quart 3% peroxide
1/4 cup baking soda
1 tablespoon liquid hand soap

Mix everything together, and then scrub your skin or your pet's fur with the solution. Be careful not to get the solution in your eyes and ears or your pet's eyes and ears. Let the solution soak in for about five minutes. Rinse. Repeat if necessary. (It will probably be necessary!)

Skunks spray their stinky smell only when they feel they are in danger and they have no way to escape. Usually, before skunks spray, they give several warnings. They will growl and stamp their feet or fluff their tail. If none of those actions chases the danger away, skunks will lift their tails and spray their scent on the animal or person. That usually does the trick. Skunks can squirt their spray about 15 feet. They have enough scent in their glands to spray five or six times.

NYAH, NYAH.

SMELLY FACT
Skunks have a high tolerance for snake venom.

Porcupines

Porcupines are not only sticky, they're stinky! Porcupines are rodents, just like mice and hamsters, but they are much larger than those animals. They can weigh as much as 60 pounds. There's only one rodent in North America that is larger than a porcupine . . . can you guess what it is? A beaver!

Porcupines are chubby little guys with short legs. They are about 25 to 30 inches long and can weigh more than 30 pounds. They are covered with sharp, pointed quills.

Have you ever wondered how mama porcupines give birth to baby porcupines that have sharp quills? Nature has a clever way of taking care of that problem. When baby porcupines are born, their quills are soft like thick hairs, but within a few minutes after the baby porcupine is born, the quills become stiff and hard and they stay that way for the rest of the porcupine's life.

Porcupines are vegetarians. They don't eat any meat, but they do like salt. Because most plants don't have much salt in them, porcupines need to find other ways to get the salt they need. They often lick the handles on garden tools to get the salt from the human sweat on the handles.

Porcupines have great senses of smell, hearing, and taste, but they have poor eyesight. Some people think porcupines can shoot their quills like arrows, but they can't. The quills are attached to the porcupine's skin and come out very easily. When porcupines feel threatened, they shake their tail at the enemy and if the quills make contact, they stick like glue. The really dangerous thing about porcupine quills is that once they make contact with another animal or human's skin, they begin to dig deeper and deeper into the skin. That's why it's best to remove porcupine quills as soon as possible.

When they are threatened, porcupines will first chatter their teeth to scare predators away. If that doesn't work, a porcupine produces a strong skunk-like odor, which is very unpleasant. If the porcupine is in a small space, the odor can be strong enough to make a human being's eyes and nose water.

SMELLY FACT

The average porcupine has about 30,000 quills. Porcupines are excellent swimmers because their quills are hollow and keep them afloat.

Tasmanian Devils

These little guys not only smell bad when they get stressed, they also scream, snort, and snarl. Then their ears turn purplish-red. Whew! Now you know how they got their name! Tasmanian devils are marsupials, which mean they carry their young in a pouch like a kangaroo. They grow to be up to 30 inches long and can weigh more than 20 pounds.

The Tasmanian Devil has powerful, bone-crunching jaws, much stronger than dog jaws, but it is not a picky eater. It prefers dead animals it finds in the jungle or on the road. Tasmanian Devils even eat the dead animals' fur!

If you'd like to actually hear the creepy sound a Tasmanian Devil makes, you can visit this Web site: www.parks.tas.gov.au/wildlife/mammals/devil.html.

Many people keep ferrets as pets. Ferrets are mischievous and active and they're a lot of fun to watch. Unfortunately, ferrets have an odor that is not very pleasant.

Sometimes, a ferret's owner will try to eliminate its odor by bathing it. But that won't work because the odor is caused by musk glands under the ferret's skin. In fact, if a ferret is bathed too much, the natural oils in the animal's skin can be washed away and the musk glands can work even harder to replace the oils. That can make the ferret smell worse than it normally would.

The best way to minimize the odor is to keep a ferret's coat clean by brushing it and by bathing it only when it sheds its fur.

SMELLY FACT
Ferrets have smelly ear wax, so their ears have to be cleaned regularly.

Turkey Vultures

Most birds don't have a very good sense of smell. They rely much more on their sense of sight. But a few birds, like the turkey vulture, are different. They have a very good sense of smell and they use it to locate food—mainly dead animals on the ground.

Turkey vultures are large birds. Their wingspan can be as much as 6 feet! They fly beautifully, but they're not very graceful on their feet. Because turkey vultures eat dead animals that are decaying on the ground, it is easy for predators to sneak up on them while they're eating. But the predators are usually sorry when they try to attack a turkey vulture because these birds have a disgusting way of chasing predators away—they vomit on them. *Bleeeah!*

And if you think that's disgusting, wait until you read this: When turkey vultures get very hot, they poop on their own legs to cool themselves. It sounds awful, but it works.

These strange birds also have a very unusual digestive system. They can eat the nastiest, rottingest, stinkiest dead animal on the road without getting sick. That's because they have chemicals in their stomachs that kill all the harmful bacteria in the rotting meat. That sounds disgusting to us human beings, but turkey vultures help keep the environment clean and reduce the spread of disease. They may not be pretty or have very nice habits, but turkey vultures are important to all of us.

SMELLY FACT
Turkey vultures don't build nests. They just lay their eggs on the ground or in rocky crevices.

Kakapos

The Kakapo is an endangered New Zealand parrot with some very unusual characteristics. For example, it's the only parrot that cannot fly. However, it is an excellent climber and spends much of its time climbing from tree limb to tree limb in search of food.

It is also the only parrot that is nocturnal. That means it is active at night rather than during the day. In fact, in the language of the Maori people, the name Kakapo means "night parrot."

The Kakapo has a very unusual odor. Most people describe the odor as sweet and musty. This odor can be a problem for the Kakapo because predators know its smell, and the unusual odor makes the bird easy to find. Today, there are only about a hundred Kakapos left in the world.

Even though kakapos can't fly, they do use their wings for balance and to slow them down when they jump from tree limbs.

SMELLY FACT
The Kakapo is the heaviest parrot in the world.

The Kakapo has one other very strange characteristic. Instead of singing or chirping, the Kakapo makes a very weird sound. If you'd like to hear the sound a Kakapo makes, visit this Web site: www.kakaporecovery.org.nz/kakapo/behaviour.html.

SMELLY FACTS

Deer don't like the smell of garlic.
Rabbits don't like the smell of marigolds.
Roaches don't like the smell of catnip.
Cats don't like the smell of citrus fruit.
Ants don't like the smell of vinegar.
Fleas don't like the smell of peppermint.
Mosquitoes don't like the smell of the castor bean plant.
Silverfish don't like the smell of cloves.
Moles don't like the smell of used cat litter (who does?).

Mink Frogs

Mink frogs don't like to be disturbed. When a predator (or a human!) bothers them, mink frogs produce an unpleasant musky, odor. The odor smells very similar to the odor a mink produces . . . which is how this frog got its name. Some people describe the smell as "rotten onions."

It's easy to tell a male mink frog from a female. Each has a flat, round organ on the side of its head called a tympanum. This works very much like a human eardrum. The male's tympanum is much larger than his eye. The female's tympanum is about the same size as her eye.

Mink frogs spend their lives in or near the water. When threatened, they like to hide in water lilies or other nearby plants for protection. They prefer colder waters and are found in the northern United States and Canada.

SMELLY FACT
Female mink frogs can lay up to 4,000 eggs at a time.

YOU SMELL FAMILIAR. ARE WE RELATED?

Stinkpot Turtles

The scientific name for stinkpot turtles is *Sternotherus odoratus*. And there's a good reason why the word *odor* is in its name. When a stinkpot turtle feels threatened or annoyed, it produces a smelly, yellow fluid from four glands near the bottom of its shell.

Besides being stinky, stinkpot turtles have a nasty habit of biting when they're upset. If you see one, it's probably a good idea to stay away and not try to pick it up. Male stinkpots are a little larger than females, but neither gets much larger than 5 inches (13 centimeters) long.

Stinkpot turtles spend most of their lives in the water. When they are searching for food, they will often walk along the bottom of a pond or slow-moving stream instead of swimming.

When the water temperature drops, stinkpot turtles bury themselves underwater in the mud and hibernate. In the spring, the female lays up to nine eggs at a time, which hatch in two to three months.

Smelly Bugs

Not all smelly animals are mammals, marsupials, or birds. There are a lot of smelly insects too.

Stinkbugs are probably the best-known smelly insects. Many stinkbugs are brightly colored and easy to see. This is a warning to predators that they are not good to eat. If the warning doesn't work, all stinkbugs have the ability to release a foul-smelling liquid. They do this to keep birds and other predators from eating them. Some stinkbugs are a flat, dull color; others are brightly colored and easy to see.

SMELLY JOKE

Do stinkbugs listen to the radio?
No! They watch smelly-vision!

I STINK, THEREFORE I AM.

Look at the different colors and patterns on these smelly bugs:

SMELLY RIDDLE

Why did the judge tell the stinkbug to sit down? Because he was out of odor.

Smelly Bugs

Here are images of some of the thousands of kinds of bugs that smell bad. Have you seen (or smelled) any of these little guys around your house?

Harlequin Bug

Spined Soldier Bug

Where does the smelly bugs' stinky stuff come from?

Every smelly bug has its own ways of releasing its smelly odor. Some squeeze it out of their bodies, some squirt it, and some make it bubble out. Below are photos of a smelly bug named Proxys punctulatus. You can see the bug's stink gland opening.

Darkling Beetles

These creatures are the "class clowns" of the beetle world. In fact, they're sometimes called clown beetles. When they are threatened, they will stand on their heads and point their rear ends at anything that comes close. It's crazy! The Darkling Beetle does this as a warning. If the intruder does not get the message, the Darkling Beetle will release a foul-smelling liquid that almost always chases an intruder away. That's why they're sometimes also called stink beetles.

The Cactus Longhorn Beetle looks very similar to the Darkling Beetle and lives in the same area, but it doesn't smell bad. This little guy is pretty smart. If a predator comes sniffing around, the Cactus Longhorn Beetle will stick its backside up in the air just like a Darkling Beetle. And that's usually enough of a warning for any predator that remembers getting squirted by the Darkling Beetle's nasty stuff.

You're looking at the face of a Bombardier Beetle. They are amazing creatures. When they are threatened, they have the ability to mix two chemicals together in their bodies and squirt the mixture out of their bodies at a predator. The amazing thing is that as the chemicals mix inside the beetle's body, they reach the temperature of boiling water! Bombardier beetles aren't really stinky insects, but their boiling brew keeps them safe from any creatures that might want to have them for dinner.

When the Bombardier Beetle squirts its boiling hot liquid, it doesn't squirt it out all at once. It actually pumps the liquid out in a series of quick bursts— about 500 bursts per second!

Ahhh... That's better...

ICE WATER

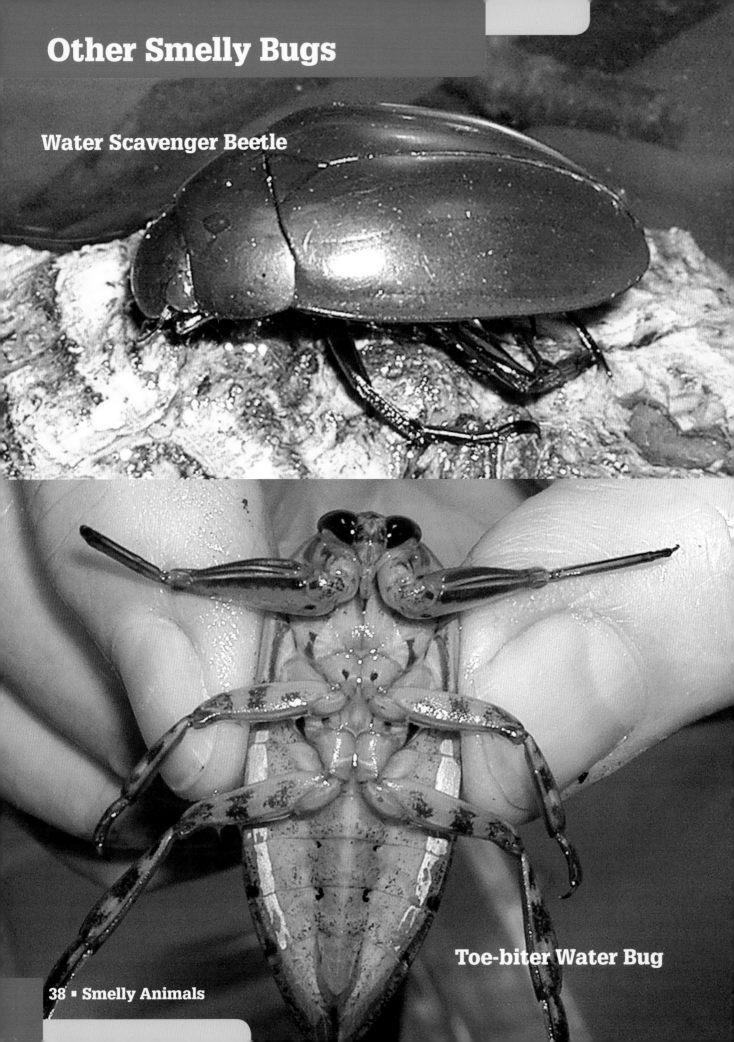

Other Smelly Bugs

Water Scavenger Beetle

Toe-biter Water Bug

BUG POETRY

To us humans, some bugs smell quite frightful
And squirt stinky stuff to be spiteful,
But to a bug's nose
It might smell like a rose
And they find the smell simply delightful.

Caterpillar Hunter or Firey Searcher Beetle

Golden Egg Bug

Assassin Bugs

Assassin Bugs are related to stinkbugs and they also produce smelly scents, but their scents are not quite as stinky as the stinkbugs'. They are called Assassin Bugs because they hide and wait until they can surprise their prey.

The White-Eyed Assassin Bug has two large dots on its back that look like big white eyes.

The Red-Eyed Assassin Bug has similar markings, but the dots are red.

White-Eyed Assassin

Red-Eyed Assassin

This Assassin Bug waited until a cricket came hopping by and then pounced on it. Assassin Bugs kill their prey by injecting it with a liquid that dissolves the animal's insides. Then they use their sharp, straw-like mouthparts to suck up the creature's insides. It's similar to the way a spider kills its prey.

BUG POETRY

Assassin Bugs are very clever.
They will sit and wait forever.
They have patience and here's why:
They know there's a meal nearby.

Ladybugs

Ladybugs are also called Lady Beetles or Ladybird Beetles. These little guys (oops . . . I mean "girls") are a welcomed sight in gardens because they love to eat the insects that destroy plants. They especially like aphids. In fact, ladybug larva will often eat their weight in aphids each day. Some companies raise and sell ladybugs to farmers and gardeners because the little critters do such a good job of eating harmful insects.

There is something about ladybugs that is not very lady-like. When threatened, they squeeze blood out of their bodies. This is called "reflex bleeding." Besides being a weird yellow-orange color, their blood has a nasty smell. That's usually enough to chase away a predator.

And there's one other bad thing about ladybugs. If their blood gets on your clothes or furniture, it leaves a stain. Considering all that, it's not a good idea to upset a ladybug.

SMELLY FACT

Ladybugs don't bite, but they have been known to nibble. They're not trying to hurt you when they nibble. They're just investigating the unusual feel of your skin.

When it gets cold outside, ladybugs will often huddle together in a warm place, like a sunny window. Sometimes ladybugs also group together to eat if there is a lot of food or if they are looking for a mate.

Look at these photos of different kinds of ladybugs. Notice how they have different colorations and markings.

Ants

Most ants are tiny, but they're not timid. When an ant discovers an intruder threatening the anthill, it will fight to the death. Some ants use their powerful jaws called mandibles to attack the intruder. Other ants will sting the unwanted guest. But some ants actually spray a toxic liquid onto the intruder when they feel threatened. The liquid is called formic acid and it smells really bad. You will probably never smell the ants' formic acid because chances are you will never get close enough. But scientists have known for hundreds of years about the unpleasant smell that some ants can produce.

SMELLY FACT

In the 1960s, scientists began making large amounts of formic acid in chemical plants. They discovered that it was effective in killing the bacteria in the food they fed to cattle.

I'M NOT FIGHTING – THIS GUY... HE STINKS!

Some ants have a very strong smell when they are crushed. Odorous house ants smell like rotten coconuts. The Citronella Ant smells "lemony."

SMELLY JOKE
What kind of ants smell the best? Deodor-ants!

Cockroaches

Cockroach. Just the word makes your skin crawl, doesn't it? Besides being creepy, cockroaches produce a terrible smell. In areas where there are many roaches nesting together, the smell is very strong. Roaches need water to survive, so they often live and hide around sinks, bathtubs, and water heaters. They are most active at night and prefer temperatures above 70 degrees Fahrenheit.

SMELLY FACT

There are fifty-five species of cockroaches in the United States. None of these cockroaches bite.

Now, here's the weirdest thing about cockroaches: They can live without their heads for at least nine days. Really! If a cockroach has a good meal and then loses its head, it can live for about nine days. It doesn't need its head to breathe because it breathes through tiny holes in its body called spiracles. And its blood doesn't move through its body the same way blood moves through a human body, so it doesn't bleed to death. The only thing creepier than a cockroach is a headless cockroach!

Would you like to see a nice closeup video of cockroach eating? Visit this Web site: http://everest.ento.vt.edu/~carroll/insect_video_feeding.html#cockroachvideo.

HMM... NOW WHERE DID I LEAVE MY HEAD?

.. OVER HERE!

SMELLY JOKE
What happened to the cockroach that got stuck in a bottle? It became a corkroach.

Cockroaches

Would you like a cockroach for a pet? Most cockroaches don't make very good pets, but there are a few species that universities and laboratories collect and raise for study. It takes special permission from the United States Department of Agriculture to buy and raise these cockroaches. Why? Because they could become a real problem if they got loose and started reproducing and spreading into our homes and businesses. The USDA wants to be sure that people who raise roaches know what they're doing.

The roaches below are strange and unusual—and they all smell bad.

Madagascar Hissing Cockroach

This roach, which is native to Africa, may look creepy but it doesn't bite and it's not dangerous. One of the reasons it's called a "hissing" cockroach is that it makes a hissing sound when it's handled or disturbed. It does this to scare away predators.

Madagascar Hissing Cockroach

Giant Cave Cockroach

This cockroach, which is found in Central and South America, can grow more than 3 inches (88 milllimeters) long. That's this big:

This roach loves to eat sweet things. But if you decide to keep it as a pet, you'll also have to feed it some meat every now and then. If you don't, and there's another roach nearby, it'll eat the other roach.

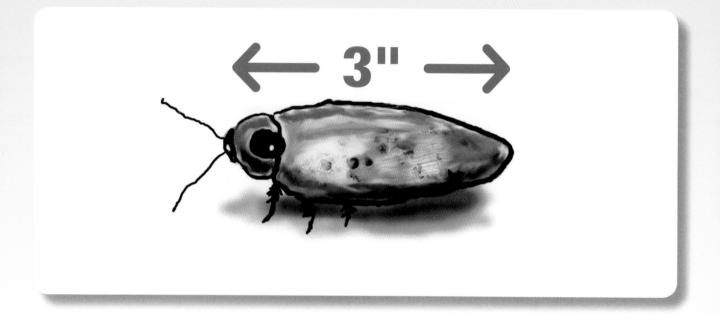

Millipedes

The word millipede means "thousand feet." They don't really have a thousand feet, but they do have a lot of them! Most millipedes have four legs on each segment of their bodies, except for the first three segments. Those parts only have two legs each. Millipedes won't bite you, but some people are allergic to the strong-smelling fluid they produce when threatened.

I'D WASH MY HANDS TOO, BUT IT WOULD TAKE ALL DAY!

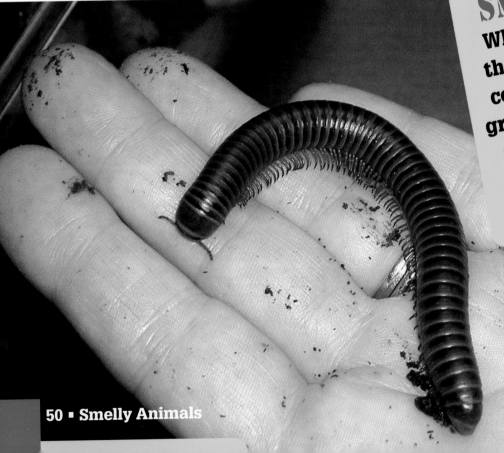

SMELLY FACT
When animals molt, they shed their outer covering so they can grow larger. Each time a millipede molts, it adds new segments and new legs.

Millipedes

If a predator gets too nosy, a millipede will squeeze some smelly fluid from between spaces in its body parts. This smell doesn't bother humans, but other animals hate it. The fluid contains the chemical cyanide, which smells like almonds. But you wouldn't want to eat a millipede. **Bleeah!**

This big guy is a Giant African Millipede. It's harmless and friendly, but it can squeeze out a yellowish, smelly liquid that will turn purple and stain your hands if you don't wash it off quickly.

Centipedes

Centipedes are related to millipedes, but they only have one pair of legs on each body segment. Believe it or not, both centipedes and millipedes are related to shrimp and crawfish. Centipedes will bite, so it's never a good idea to handle one with your bare hands.

The largest centipede inhabits the Caribbean Islands and north and west areas of South America. Its name is Scolopendra gigantea, and when fully mature it can grow to a length of 12 inches (30.5 centimeters). That's longer that this book is from top to bottom! A closely related centipede can be found in Texas and the southwestern United States and can grow to more than 10 inches (25.4 centimeters) long. Here's a picture of the Giant Desert Centipede:

If you'd like to see a close-up video of a Scolopendra gigantea centipede crawling around, visit this Website: www.nhm.ac.uk/about-us/news/2005/august/news_6293.html.

Want to know more about millipedes and centipedes? This Web site has a great quiz that you can take. Give it a try! www.funtrivia.com/quizdetails.cfm?quiz=81747.

And now: The world's largest collection of centipede jokes.

Who brings presents to all the good little centipedes? Sata-pede.

What kind of a doctor takes care of baby centipedes? A centipediatrician.

What do you call a centipede walking down the street? A centipedestrian.

Do you measure centipedes in inches? No. You measure them in centimeters.

What will you find on a centipede's report card? Centigrades.

How does a centipede decorate a table? With a centi-piece.

Why do centipedes have so many pictures of their relatives on the wall? Because they're very centi-mental.

Why do centipedes make such bad soldiers? Because when they march, they have to say "LEFT" one hundred times before they can say "RIGHT."

What's worse than having to buy gloves for an octopus? Having to buy shoes for a centipede.

SMELLY FACT
Centipedes can live as long as six years.

Earwigs

Do you know how earwigs got their name? People used to believe that earwigs would crawl into the ears of a person who was sleeping and would attach themselves to the person's brain, which would make the person go crazy. Of course, that idea is ridiculous and impossible. The human ear has an eardrum that prevents anything from crawling into a person's head. And those tickly little legs would probably make the person wake up anyway.

Even though they're harmless, earwigs do look pretty scary. They can give a slight pinch with their claw-like tail, but it doesn't hurt very badly. The worst things about earwigs is the yellowish-brown liquid they squeeze out of their scent glands. It's really smelly!

Earwigs usually hide during the day and become active at night. They can fly but almost never do. In fact, they don't even walk much. They prefer to hide in boxes and baskets and on flowers and hitch a ride when those things are moved.

I'M NOT GOING IN THERE. IT'S TOO DARK.

There's not much nice to say about bed bugs. Bedbugs smell bad and drink human blood. The good news is that they're small so it only takes about five minutes for them to fill up and they don't have to feed very often. Some bedbugs can live for more than a year without feeding.

Bedbugs produce a liquid that is easy to smell, especially when there are large numbers of them in one place. It smells sweet like raspberries or soda pop syrup. Unfortunately, the liquid can stain sheets and mattresses. Bedbugs also have a nasty habit of shedding their outer skins and leaving them on the bed sheets.

Bedbugs used to be a big problem in the United States, but since insecticides (bug killing chemicals) became popular in many homes, bedbugs aren't as common as they used to be. Bedbugs are only about this big: ●

They're normally brown, but they turn a nice reddish-brown after they suck your blood! Yikes!

SMELLY FACT
Bedbugs can't fly, but they do run fast. Bedbugs are not known to spread any diseases.

SMELLY TONGUE TWISTER
A bunch of bad bedbugs bit a baby bird, but the baby bird's brother bit the bedbugs back.

Giant Mesquite Bugs

The Giant Mesquite Bug loves to eat mesquite plants. Actually, they suck the sap from the plants. They are the largest of the true bugs. A "true bug" is one that has a piercing or sucking mouth part. Some true bugs like the Giant Mesquite Bug suck the sap from trees, while others use their mouth parts to punch holes in skin. It's common to see several Giant Mesquite Bugs feeding off of a single mesquite tree.

Giant Mesquite Bugs aren't the only creatures that get food from the mesquite tree. Human beings do, too! Native Americans in the southwestern United States eat the bright yellow mesquite bean pods that grow on the tree. And people who like to barbeque add mesquite wood to the fire to give meat a wonderful sweet taste.

PARDNER... THIS MESQUITE PLANT AIN'T BIG ENOUGH FOR BOTH OF US.

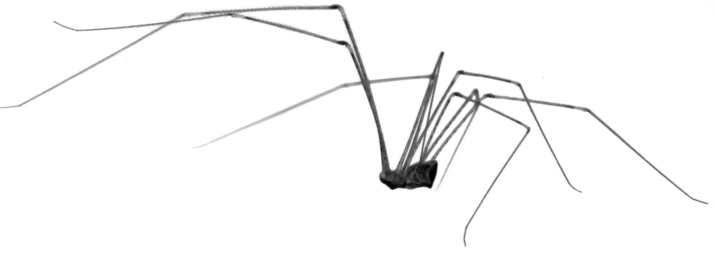

Daddy Long Legs

Daddy Long Legs have eight legs, and they are arachnids, but they're not spiders. Spiders have two body parts, but Daddy Long Legs only have one. They got their name because most of the animal is legs! Inside small openings in each of the legs, there are many little sensors that tell the Daddy Long Legs where it is, what other creatures might be in the area, and if there's some food nearby. Daddy Long Legs will eat almost anything, including snails, worms, and other Daddy Long Legs.

Daddy Long Legs should probably be called Daddy Loose Legs because their legs will fall off easily if they are handled. And if they lose a leg, it does not grow back. Having loose legs can help a Daddy Long Legs escape if a predator is trying to eat it.

When a Daddy Long Legs feels threatened, it will wave two of its legs in the air. If that doesn't work, it squeezes out a nasty-smelling liquid that discourages predators.

SMELLY FACT

When a Daddy Long Legs loses a leg, the leg keeps twitching for several minutes. That helps to confuse a predator so the Daddy Long Legs can escape.

Remember...
wave first,
then squeeze.

Yes, daddy.

Vinegaroons

Vinegaroons, also known as *whipscorpions*, are usually found in the southwestern United States. Vinegaroons got their names because when they are frightened, they can squirt a liquid from their tail that smells like vinegar. The spray has an acid in it that is toxic to small predators. The pointy "stinger" is not really a stinger at all. It is the tube from which they spray the smelly liquid. It is covered with sensitive hairs that tell the Vinegaroon when another creature is nearby.

Vinegaroons look scary, but they are harmless to humans. Because they have bad eyesight, Vinegaroons depend on their sense of touch to find food. They use their claws to catch roaches, crickets, and other small bugs. But they don't eat the bugs right away. Instead, they take them back to their burrows and eat them there.

The chemical that gives the Vinegaroon its "vinegary" smell is acetic acid, which is one of the main ingredients in aspirin.

The Angoumois Grain Moth

The Angoumois Grain Moth likes to eat corn. After the corn has been picked and is stored, the female Angoumois Grain Moth lays her eggs in the corn kernels. When the larvae hatch, the little pests dig into the kernels and begin to eat. And as they do, they make the corn smell terrible.

Angoumois Grain Moth

The Luna Moth and the Lesser Emperor Moth

A male Luna Moth can smell a female Luna Moth from as far as five miles away. But the male Lesser Emperor Moth has an even more incredible sense of smell. It can smell a female Lesser Emperor Moth more than six miles away!

Luna Moth

Zebra Swallowtail Caterpillars

How would you like to spend every waking minute of every day eating? That's what the Zebra Swallowtail Caterpillar does. In fact, that's what most caterpillars do. The Zebra Swallowtail Caterpillar likes to feed on a plant called the "Paw Paw" plant (Asimina triloba).

Because caterpillars are so slow-moving and soft, they make great food for birds and other small predators. But the Zebra Swallowtail Caterpillar has bright markings that warn predators to stay away. If a predator gets too close, the Zebra Swallowtail Caterpillar exposes an orange gland called an osmeterium, which has a very nasty odor and taste. Predators soon learn that they don't want to have this smelly little guy for dinner.

SMELLY FACT
Zebra Swallowtail Caterpillars are cannibals! They will eat each other!

DID SOMEBODY SAY, "PAW PAW?"

This is the Southeastern Lubber Grasshopper. This guy can squeeze a smelly, bubbly liquid out of its body that repels hungry predators. As an extra measure, as it creates the smelly liquid, it makes a loud hissing noise that frightens and confuses potential predators. And finally, as an extra disgusting measure, the Lubber can spit up a nasty brown liquid called "tobacco juice" that is sure to make any predator look for something else to eat for dinner.

There are many kinds of grasshoppers. In Japan, people love to eat the Rice Field Grasshopper. They make a dish called inago, which is Rice Field Grasshopper that has been fried and seasoned. Yum! Sounds good, doesn't it?

SMELLY FACT

In 2003 in the country of Sudan, thousands of people were taken to the hospital when grasshoppers swarmed and gave off such a terrible smell that people had trouble breathing.

Gee... We thought we smelled pretty good.

Walking Sticks

Walking Sticks are well named because they look just like . . . um . . . walking sticks. They can be brown or dark green and their shape makes them very difficult to see in trees and on other plants. They don't eat anything but leaves and plants, so they are not a threat to humans. They are fun to watch and lots of people keep them as pets.

Some Walking Sticks look like twigs and others look like leaves. Although most of the different kinds of Walking Sticks are easy to care for and make fine pets, there are a few that defend themselves by spraying a liquid that can burn your eyes. Others spray a liquid with an unpleasant odor.

If you look carefully, you may see a Walking Stick gently swaying back and forth like a small twig or leaf being blown by the wind. This is a very clever form of camouflage which makes it difficult for predators to spot them.

SMELLY FACT
There are more than 3,000 different kinds of Walking Sticks.

Walking Sticks

There's something strange about this picture. Can you see what it is? The Walking Stick is missing a leg!

Walking Sticks, like all insects, have their skeletons on the outside of their bodies. In order to grow, they have to shed their skeleton "skins" from time to time. If a Walking Stick loses a leg in a fight or because a predator is trying to catch it, it can always grow a new one . . . as long as it is still growing. Once a Walking Stick is fully grown, however, it can no longer grow a new leg. This Walking Stick obviously lost its leg after it was fully grown. But it's OK, it gets along just fine with its other five legs. And it can always find something interesting to crawl on, as you can see.

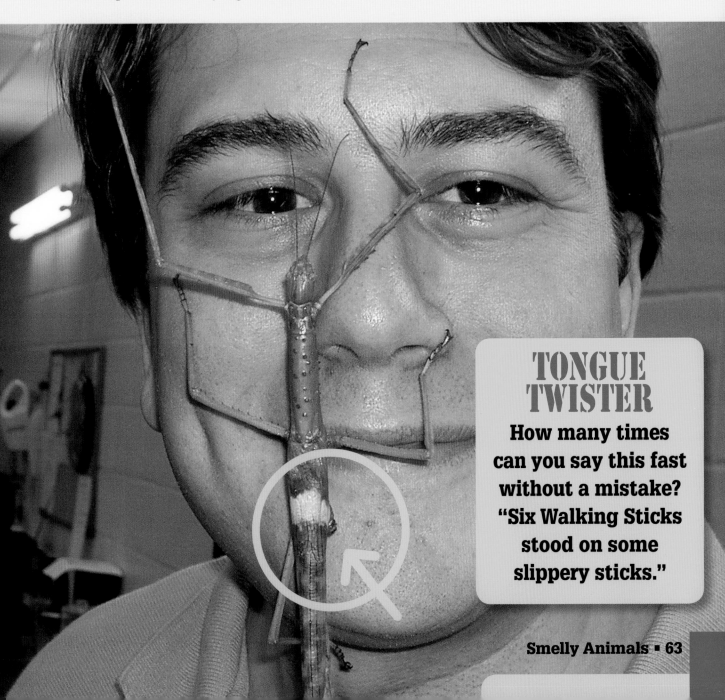

TONGUE TWISTER

How many times can you say this fast without a mistake? "Six Walking Sticks stood on some slippery sticks."

Underwater Stinkers

P EE-*YEW!* Fish really smell bad. Um, but they smell good. Well, not really good, but here's a better explanation . . .

Fish don't have noses like humans because they smell things in the water, not in the air. Like humans, fish have nostrils, but inside the nostrils are nasal sacs with folds that can sense small amounts of chemicals as water passes over them.

The more folds, the better the fish can smell. Some catfish have about 140 folds.

Largemouth bass have only 10 to 13 folds so they can't smell as many things in the water.

Scientists have done experiments in which they mixed one part of a compound into ten billion parts of water and the catfish were able to smell that one part.

Sharks also have an excellent sense of smell and can detect blood in the water from almost a mile away. Whales and dolphins aren't as lucky. Compared to fish, sea mammals don't have as good a sense of smell.

When it's time for salmon to spawn (reproduce), they always return to the stream in which they were born. When the young salmon hatch, they swim out to sea. For years, scientists wondered how the salmon found the same stream every year. Recent experiments indicate that salmon use their incredible sense of smell to find their "home" stream. It's a little like growing up near a paper mill or a bakery. If you were lost, the smell would help you find your way.

Most people love the taste of fresh salmon. Salmon use their incredible sense of smell to protect them from getting caught and eaten. In one experiment, scientists found that salmon could detect just one part of human skin in eighty billion parts of water. When they put that solution into a stream,

the salmon stopped migrating for up to thirty minutes. We humans have a smell caused by chemicals in our bodies and salmon know that our smell means danger. Adult men pose the strongest "danger" smell to salmon. Woman and children have smells that aren't as strong.

SNIFF

NEXT YEAR, I'M BRINGING A MAP!

SNIFF

SNIFF

Part III

Smelly Plants

The Corpse Plant

The Corpse Plant grows from a large underground root that can weigh as much as 170 pounds. The plant usually grows about 6 feet tall, but one plant in Bonn, Germany, grew to almost 9 feet tall. Most people agree that the corpse flower is the largest flower in the plant kingdom.

Scientists at the University of California at Davis have been studying one particular Corpse Plant for years. According to one of the scientists, the odor from the plant sometimes smells like dead fish and at other times smells like a rotting pumpkin.

The seeds of the Corpse Plant were first collected in Sumatra in 1878 by Italian botanists who brought them to Europe. When the first bloom in captivity appeared in England's Royal Botanical Garden 1889, large crowds gathered to see the strange and smelly flower.

Want to know more about this stinky plant?
Visit: www.huntington.org/BotanicalDiv/TitanArum.htm.

SMELLY FACT
The Corpse Plant only blooms two or three times in its forty-year lifetime.

The Mediterranean is a large body of water that separates Europe from Africa. Some small islands in the Mediterranean are home to the Dead Horse Arum. As you can guess from the name, this plant smells terrible. Scientists have learned that part of the reason for the smell is a group of chemicals in the plant called oligosulfides. That's a big name for some very smelly chemicals.

Can you guess where else scientists have found those smelly chemicals? In dead animals! That's right. Blowflies lay their eggs in rotting meat. But blowflies can't tell the difference between the smell of a dead animal and the smell of a Dead Horse Arum. The Dead Horse Arum tricks the blowfly into thinking it is laying its eggs in a dead animal. As the blowfly lays its eggs, some of the pollen from the Dead Horse Arum sticks to the fly's legs.

Then the fly leaves and the next time it lays its eggs in another Dead Horse Arum, it fertilizes the plant and that makes it possible for the plant to reproduce. Pretty clever plant, huh?

SMELLY FACT

The Dead Horse Arum is about 25 degrees Fahrenheit warmer than most other plants. This warmth helps to send the stinky smell into the air so flies can smell it more easily.

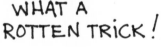
WHAT A ROTTEN TRICK!

The Carrion Flower

ike the Dead Horse Aurum, the Carrion Flower smells like rotting meat. This plant is native to South Africa and the deep red color of its flower helps to give bugs the impression that what they're landing on is dead flesh.

And just to make sure that flies are completely fooled, the Carrion Flower has fine "hairs" on its surface that are much like the hairs on an animal.

The Carrion Flower is known by many names. Here are a few:

> Zulu Giant
> Hairy Starfish Flower
> Star Cactus
> Starfish Cactus

The last two names are not accurate because the plant really isn't a cactus. It just looks like one.

ANOTHER ROTTEN TRICK!

Dutchman's Pipes

There are many types of Dutchman's Pipe plants. They all get their name from the plant's S-shaped flower that looks like the kind of old pipes that men used to smoke. You may have read about the fictional mystery detective Sherlock Holmes, who used to smoke a pipe shaped like that. The flowers of these plants can be yellowish-green, purplish-brown, red, cream-colored, or multicolored, but regardless of the color, they all smell bad.

Dutchman's Pipe vines have large leaves and the plants grow quickly. Many home gardeners grow the plants on fences or trellises as a screen.

The Lifesaver Plant

Many people call this a "lifesaver plant" because it looks as if a little lifesaver has been placed in the middle of a tiger-striped star. The flowers bloom among the long, sticky spines of the plant. Even though the Lifesaver Plant looks like a cactus, it's not. It belongs to a group of plants called succulents. Succulents are plants that store water. The Lifesaver Plant is native to Africa and Arabia and produces a very stinky smell that attracts flies and other pollinating insects.

There are more than sixty varieties of this plant, and you can see wonderful pictures of them at this Web site: www.succulent-plant.com/huernia.html. Scientists named these plants after Justus Heurnius, who was a Dutch missionary and amateur botanist in the seventeenth century.

SMELLY FACT

Insects see colors differently than we do. Through many insects' eyes, the color white has a bright, attractive glow. That's why many flowers that rely on insects for pollination often have some white spots or shapes on them.

MRS HEURNIUS

THEY NAMED A STINKY PLANT AFTER ME. AREN'T YOU PROUD?

The Lantern Stinkhorn

Imagine a mushroom that pokes out of the ground looking like a horn with a top covered in black, slimy ooze full of tiny mushroom spores. Oh yes, and imagine the whole thing smells like dog poop. YUCK! Well, that's a good description of a Lantern Stinkhorn.

The Lantern Stinkhorn starts out as a small egg-shaped object that grows underground. When it becomes about the size of a golf ball, it breaks open and the "horn" pushes its way above ground very quickly.

Flies assume that the stinky smell is food and they crowd around the slimy top of the Lantern Stinkhorn looking for something to eat. When they don't find any food, they fly off, but not before some of the spores in that sticky goop get stuck on the fly's legs. When the fly dies and falls to the ground, the spores fall with it. If the soil, water, and light conditions are just right, the spores will grow into a new Lantern Stinkhorn.

The Starfish Fungus

The Starfish Fungus is related to the Lantern Stinkhorn, but it looks and smells very different. Instead of growing tall and thin, the Starfish Fungus spreads out into a shape that looks like a starfish. Like the Lantern Stinkhorn, the starfish fungus has a black, slimy goop that is filled with spores, but the Starfish Fungus smells more like rotting meat than dog poop.

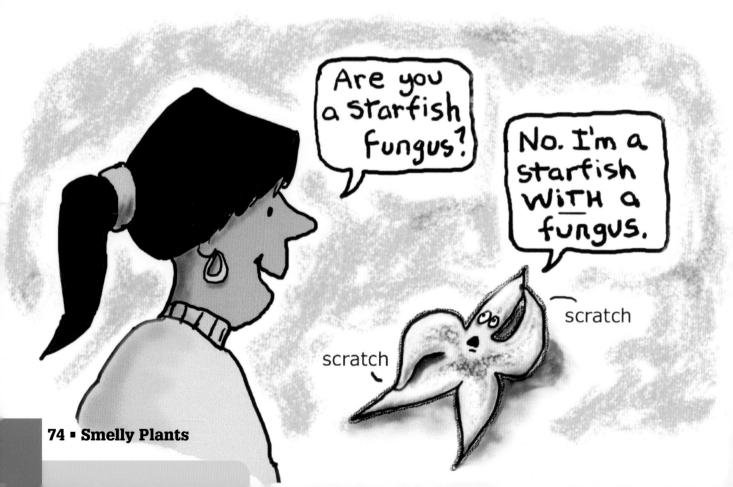

TONGUE TWISTER
How many times can you say this tongue twister in ten seconds? "I think some kids squished Stinky Squids."

The Stinky Squid was originally a tropical fungus, but it can now be found in many parts of the United States, even where it gets cold during the winter. Like the Stinkhorn and Starfish Fungus, the Stinky Squid begins as a small egg-shaped growth beneath the ground. It absorbs moisture and expands until it bursts open and sends stalks up above ground. The Stinky Squid has three or four orange-red "tentacles" that produce the spores.

Look at the picture. Doesn't it look like the plant has little tentacles? Some people also think the "tentacles" look like a crab's claw.

Like the Stinkhorn and Starfish fungi, the Stinky Squid also has a smelly goop that contains spores. Flies that visit the Stinky Squid spread the spores.

Smelly Plants ▪ 75

The Stink Currant

Stink Currants are found in the northwest portion of the United States from California to Alaska. This plant is called a Stink Currant because the leaves give off a very nasty odor when they are crushed. The plant is actually a member of the gooseberry family and people use the berries to make pies and jam. Fortunately, the berries don't stink.

Some of the plants in the currant family have funny first names. Here are some examples:

Wax Currant

Stink Currant

Prickly Currant

Pioneer Gooseberry

Devil's Dung

This plant with the very unpleasant name is native to Iran, Afghanistan, and the northern part of India. There are many historical records of the milky sap of the plant being used in cooking in ancient Greece and Rome. It seems that once it's fried, the strong, sickening smell of the sap becomes a little easier on the nose.

The sap makes an excellent insect repellent (and people repellent, too!) and there are stories of people putting the plant in their shoes to repel snakes.

The plant has also been used for centuries to treat a number of medical conditions, including asthma, whooping cough, and bronchitis.

Dude! Your shoes reek!

The Sundew

Many of the plants in this book attract insects with their colors, shapes, or smells. They do this so the insects will help spread the plants' pollen or spores. The Sundew plant is different. It uses its smell to attract insects for a different reason . . . it wants to eat them!

The leaves of the Sundew plant have little points with drops of liquid on them that look like dew. Insects are attracted by the odor of the liquid, but when they land on the plant, they get stuck in the sticky stuff. The Sundew senses the insect's movement and slowly begins to close on the bug. In a little while, the leaves close completely and the plant begins to

make chemicals that kill the bug and disintegrate the bug's body. Then the plant absorbs the minerals from the dead bug's body. The leaves are like the plant's stomach!

SMELLY FACT
Plants that generate extra heat to help spread their odors are called exothermic.

The Durian Fruit

The Durian Fruit is as big as your head and it's covered with large spikes. And it really smells bad. Some restaurants and subways in Asia will not let anyone in if they have Durian Fruit with them. And why would anyone have such a smelly fruit with them anyway? Because some people love the taste of Durian Fruit.

In 2003, an airline in Australia delayed a flight for hours because the baggage handlers smelled a terrible smell in the cargo area of the jet. When they took a closer look, they found a box of Durian Fruit had been placed onboard. The whole aircraft was beginning to smell. One airline worker said he could smell the single box of Durian Fruit from 50 feet away.

SMELLY FACT
The flowers of the Durian tree are pollinated by bats!

The Noni Fruit (Indian Mulberry)

The Noni Fruit is about the size of a potato. Some people say it smells like burnt rubber—and it tastes as bad as it smells.

Some people gather Noni Fruit and let it ferment. Then they drink the liquid or mix it with other juice or water. The fermented fruit doesn't smell as bad as the ripe fruit, but it's still not very tasty. Some native folk healers in Asia and the Hawaiian Islands believe the juice of the Noni Fruit can help treat many health problems, including heart problems, arthritis, cancer, facial blemishes, infections, diabetes, and head lice.

Most medical experts believe that the juice of the Noni Fruit is not harmful, but there's no scientific proof that it has any special health benefits.

The Skunk Cabbage

One of the first plants to appear in wet, marshy areas each spring is the Skunk Cabbage. It's easy to see because it sends up a hood-shaped growth called spathe, and it has leaves that can grow up to 4 feet long (1.3 meters). And phew! does it ever smell bad.

SMELLY FACT

The Skunk Cabbage contains a chemical that can irritate your skin. More interesting is that it can melt snow by generating heat.

I LOVE THE WAY YOU SMELL.

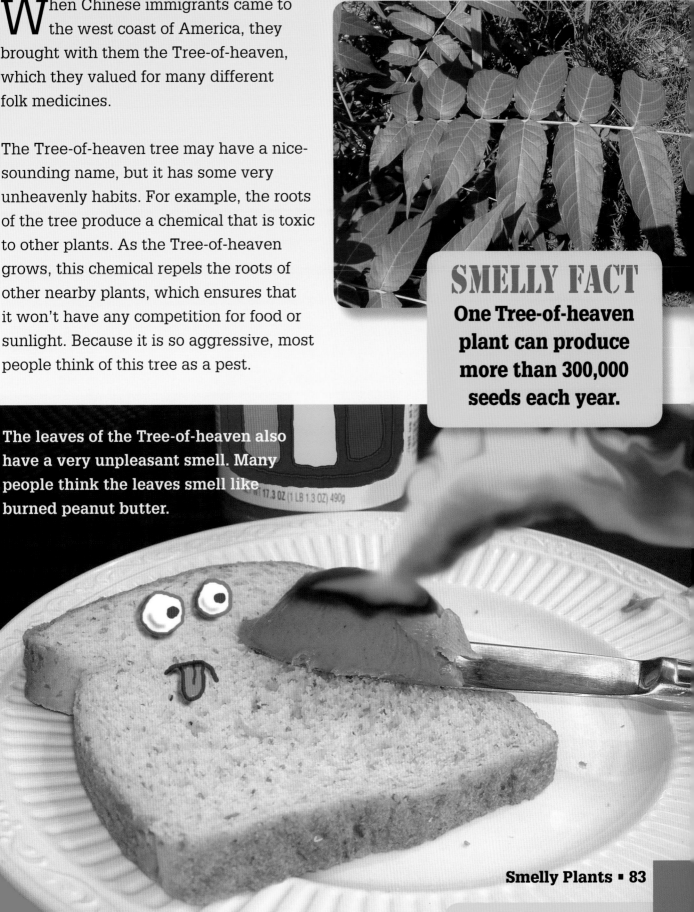

When Chinese immigrants came to the west coast of America, they brought with them the Tree-of-heaven, which they valued for many different folk medicines.

The Tree-of-heaven tree may have a nice-sounding name, but it has some very unheavenly habits. For example, the roots of the tree produce a chemical that is toxic to other plants. As the Tree-of-heaven grows, this chemical repels the roots of other nearby plants, which ensures that it won't have any competition for food or sunlight. Because it is so aggressive, most people think of this tree as a pest.

SMELLY FACT
One Tree-of-heaven plant can produce more than 300,000 seeds each year.

The leaves of the Tree-of-heaven also have a very unpleasant smell. Many people think the leaves smell like burned peanut butter.

17.3 OZ (1 LB 1.3 OZ) 490g

Part IV
More Smelly Stuff

Stinky Rocks

Yep! There are rocks that are as stinky as some of the insects and plants in this book. Rocks are made of minerals and some minerals smell really nasty.

For instance, oil shale smells like . . . crude oil.

The mineral pyrite has a strong, unpleasant sulphur odor.

Barite smells like rotten eggs.

Pumice also gives off a strong sulphur
smell when it is crushed.

Smelly Science: Stink Bombs

Scientists are now working on an honest-to-goodness stink bomb. They believe that by putting the worst smells on earth into a "stink bomb," soldiers and police won't have to use weapons as often to defend people and property from people who want to do harm. The stink bomb could just be dropped into the middle of a battlefield or a riot and the smell would be so bad that everyone involved would run the other way.

One of the problems scientists have with the idea of a stink bomb is making the smell last long enough to be effective. Because human noses get used to smells (even bad smells), scientists are working on ways to make the stink bomb continue to smell bad over time.

Another problem is how different cultures deal with smells. Something that smells good or bad to an American might not smell good or bad to people in Brazil or India. The scientists working on this project think that a mixture of smells will probably work best.

National Sense of Smell Day

National Sense of Smell Day is an annual springtime event at children's museums and science centers across the country. It focuses on our sense of smell—how it works and the important role it plays in many aspects of our daily life. In addition, schools, the media, and retailers are encouraged to join in the fun by featuring their own special events. Participating museums feature hands-on, interactive activities, including demonstrations of how the sense of smell functions in humans and animals, the connection between our senses of taste and smell, and how the sense of smell alerts us to danger, enhances our alertness, helps us to sleep, improves our mood, and much more. There are also many creative craft activities and entertainment in the form of puppet shows, storytelling, musicians, and contests.

Here are some of the museums that have celebrated National Sense of Smell Day:

**Arizona Science Center,
    Phoenix, Arizona
The Science Place, Dallas, Texas
Lawrence Hall of Science,
    Berkeley, California
Maryland Science Center,
    Baltimore, Maryland
Minnesota Children's Museum,
    St. Paul, Minnesota
Boston's Children's Museum,
    Boston, Massachusetts**

Contact your local science museum and ask them to host a smelly event in your city!

SMELLY FACT

Montpelier, Vermont, calls itself "The Rotten Sneaker Capital of the World." In 1975, the owners of a sporting goods store in town wanted to sell more sneakers, so they started the "stinky sneakers" competition. The winner gets a savings bond, money to buy new sneakers, and lots of foot deodorant. PEE-YEW!

The Sense of Smell Institute

<D>id you know that there is an organization devoted exclusively to our sense of smell? It's called the Sense of Smell Institute, and its mission is to provide information to scientists, teachers, and anyone else interested in learning more about our sense of smell.

Here's some of the great information on their Web site:

Did you know that no two people have the exact same odor-identity or "smell fingerprint?" The way you smell to others can be determined by your skin type, what you eat, and even the weather.

Your sense of smell is at work even while you're sleeping. Because the sense of smell goes into action every time we inhale, even when we are asleep, it can alert us to dangers like the smell of smoke or wake us up with the delicious aroma of fresh-brewed coffee. Research has even been done to develop an aroma alarm clock that would gently wake you up with a pleasant aroma rather than an alarm!

YOO-HOO! IT'S TIME TO WAKE UP AND SMELL THE COFFEE.

Your sense of smell is responsible for about 80 percent of what you taste. Without your sense of smell, your sense of taste is limited to only five distinct sensations: sweet, salty, sour, bitter, and the newly discovered umami, or savory sensation. All other flavors that you experience come from smell. This is why, when your nose is blocked, as by a cold, most foods seem bland or tasteless.

And here's some more information: Your sense of smell becomes stronger when you are hungry. For more smelly fun facts, visit the Sense of Smell Institute's Web site at www.senseofsmell.org.

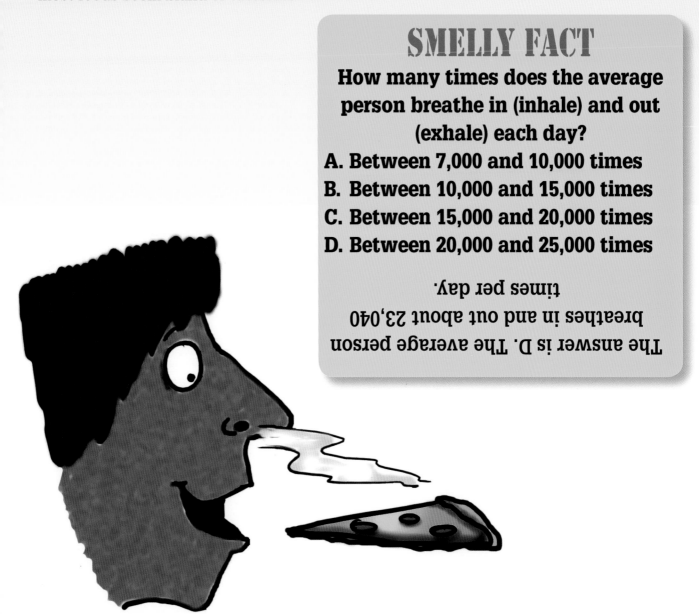

SMELLY FACT

How many times does the average person breathe in (inhale) and out (exhale) each day?

A. Between 7,000 and 10,000 times
B. Between 10,000 and 15,000 times
C. Between 15,000 and 20,000 times
D. Between 20,000 and 25,000 times

The answer is D. The average person breathes in and out about 23,040 times per day.

More Smelly Information

For more information about smelly stuff, go online!

Here are some great Web sites with lots of information about smelly plants, animals, insects, rocks, and organizations:

International Bulb Society
www.angelfire.com/ri/ixia/bulbsociety.html
This group's Web site has information and photos of some of the plants in this book.

The University of Iowa, Entymology Department
www.ent.iastate.edu/list/directory/92/vid/4
This wonderful Web site has great images of many of the smelly insects and bugs in this book.

Orkin
www.orkin.com/learning_center/kids_and_teachers.aspx
This pest control company has a cool Web site with lots of information about bugs for kids and teachers.

National Park Service
www.nature.nps.gov/biology
The U.S. National Park Service Web site describes many animals and plants. There is also a "sound" gallery that includes sounds of the national parks.

Sense of Smell Institute
www.senseofsmell.org
This organization specializes in providing information about the human sense of smell.

Monell Chemical Senses Center
www.monell.org
Monell is a company that studies smells and how they affect humans at home and in the workplace. If you have a question about smells, Monell can probably answer it.

Google
www.google.com
Do a Google Images search for any of the plants, animals, insects, or rocks in this book and you'll find a number of images of that object or creature.

Index

Index

Index

About the Author

Mike Artell has written and illustrated many children's books, and lives in Covington, Louisiana.

In addition to writing and illustrating books, Mike visits schools and libraries around the country and shares his ideas for helping children and teachers think, write, and draw more creatively. You can visit Mike on his Web site at www.mikeartell.com.